T0146776

AWAKENING THE FLAME

IGNITING YOUR POTENTIAL THROUGH THE POWER OF THE VIOLET FLAME CHAKRA

Diana Savil

BALBOA.
PRESS
A DIVISION OF HAY HOUSE

Balboa Press books may be ordered through booksellers or by contacting:

Balboa Press
A Division of Hay House
1663 Liberty Drive
Bloomington, IN 47403
www.balboapress.com
1 (877) 407-4847

Because of the dynamic nature of the Internet, any web addresses or
links contained in this book may have changed since publication and
may no longer be valid. The views expressed in this work are solely those
of the author and do not necessarily reflect the views of the publisher,
and the publisher hereby disclaims any responsibility for them.

The author of this book does not dispense medical advice or prescribe the use of
any technique as a form of treatment for physical, emotional, or medical problems
without the advice of a physician, either directly or indirectly. The intent of the
author is only to offer information of a general nature to help you
in your quest for emotional and spiritual well-being. In the event that you use
any of the information in this book for yourself, which is your constitutional
right, the author and the publisher assume no responsibility for your actions.

Image credits:
Saint-Germain image page xiii copyright Edwin Courtenay
Cover image copyright Simon Wayman
Cover photograph copyright Simon Wayman

Print information available on the last page.

ISBN: 978-1-5043-2788-6 (sc)
ISBN: 978-1-5043-2789-3 (e)

Library of Congress Control Number: 2015902403

Balboa Press rev. date: 4/10/2015

Table of Contents

Preface

When I attended Edwin Courtenay's Awakening the Violet Flame Chakra workshop on 23rd November 2013, I had no idea what a life-changing experience it would be.

Watching the energy of the Violet Flame Chakra evolve and develop, and being part of that process, has been such an amazing gift.

I am privileged to share it here, and I hope its story will touch you as it touched me. And I hope it will encourage you to seek a closer experience of it.

Welcome to your potential.

Acknowledgements

This book – indeed the whole energy of the Violet Flame Chakra – would not have come into being without the assistance of Edwin Courtenay. It was his Channelling and later presentation of the Awakening process at his workshop that introduced me to it. His continuing support as I have experienced the evolution of the Violet Flame Chakra work has been profoundly appreciated.

The further development of the work would not have been possible without the shared experiences of my "Violet Flame Chakra fellow-travellers". Thanks go to all my students, and particularly to Liz Rowlands, whose contributions played such a large part in our combined exploration.

Thanks must also go to the "Ark Ascenders": that small group to whom I offered my first Awakening, and who have loyally listened to the Channelled wisdom of Saint-Germain for several years now.

Acknowledgements would not be complete without thanking my Partner, Simon, without whose help, support, patience and understanding this book, and this work would not be reaching you. Thank you, with all my heart.

Thank you to my wonderful artists: Simon, for his cover image and Edwin for his image of the Ascended Master, Saint-Germain, both created specifically for this book.

Thanks, too, to all the wonderful people at Balboa Press, for their unfailing support and enthusiasm in enabling this venture to take physical form.

And finally, the greatest thanks of all must go to the Ascended Master, Saint-Germain. I am so privileged to be a Channel for his energy, and to have become a part of this great Awakening work. Thank you, my Master; I am honoured to serve you.

The Ascended Master, Saint-Germain
by Edwin Courtenay

A full colour version of this image can be seen at www.
violetflamechakra.com, and you can purchase a copy
for yourself at www.edwincourtenay.co.uk.

Chapter One

Imagine...

Imagine being able to connect to many dimensions and to have access to healing tools that would transform instantly, on more levels than you previously thought possible.

The energy of the Violet Flame Chakra gives you just this.

This truly amazing Gift from Saint-Germain and the Ascended Masters lifts us, changes our energy and enables us to heal and transform more rapidly and effectively than ever before.

So what is this energy, and how did it come to us?

Many of us are aware of the changes in energy which took place around the time of the winter solstice in 2012. This was a period long predicted as one of energetic shift, and much was expected of it. When the moment came, it appeared to be a bit of a damp squib. However, as time went on, it became apparent that in fact a change *had* taken place, and we were all gradually adjusting to alterations within our beings and within our lives.

For many, those adjustments included the necessary release of old energies within us which no longer served, and those processes of release manifested as difficult challenges, for some almost too much to bear. The year 2013 was a year of great struggle for many, including powerful Light Workers, who one may have thought were above such difficulties.

Part of the Divine Plan had always been that during 2014 Humanity would be gifted with powerful tools which would enable the easy release of the energies associated with these traumas and challenges.

But, observing the deep struggle in which so many Lightworkers were engaged during 2013, Saint-Germain requested that these tools be brought forward before the intended time, to assist us all.

Energetically, the year 2014 is said to begin on 1ˢᵗ November 2013, and during that month Edwin Courtenay, an international Channel and Teacher, under guidance from The Ascended Master Saint-Germain, gave workshops during which these powerful healing tools were gifted to those present, during the Awakening of their Violet Flame Chakra. Those receiving this Awakening were charged with spreading and sharing this energy and knowledge, for the benefit of all.

What is the Violet Flame Chakra?

The Violet Flame Chakra is a new energy centre within our being, through which we can connect to multi-dimensional levels of energy, and which enables us to heal and transform on those levels.

We are all capable of experiencing this Awakening, and receiving the associated healing tools.

Our Chakras

First, let us understand the nature of our "normal" chakras. These widely accepted energy centres are vortices within our energy field, or aura. Many people are familiar with the chakras associated with our physical body. Here each vortex forms a funnel shape, narrow where it is close to the body, and widening as the energy moves outwards. There are seven of these main chakras, each associated with a colour, physical organs and different qualities.

The Base Chakra

The first is our base, or root chakra, located in the perineum, at the base of the spine. This funnel of energy points downwards to the earth, and is our connection to our home planet. The colour here is red, and it is associated with our spine, bones, legs, kidneys and adrenal glands. The qualities of this chakra are physical strength and wellbeing, a strong sense of presence on the earth, and good grounding: a sense of "feet firmly on the earth".

The Sacral Chakra

The second of our main chakras is the sacral chakra, located in the lower abdomen at the level of the sacrum: the large bone at the back of the pelvic girdle. The colour associated with this chakra is orange, and it is connected to our reproductive organs, kidneys, bladder and blood. This is our creative centre – on all levels, artistic, physical (this is the level of the womb) and also of our reality. It is through this centre that we draw to ourselves situations that we choose to experience, consciously or otherwise.

The Law of Attraction dictates that whatever frequency our energy is resonating at, we will attract to ourselves situations and experiences that resonate at the same frequency. Thus if we are having a bad day, and viewing all things as difficult and obstructive, we will draw to ourselves more situations that are difficult and obstructive.

Conversely, if we are feeling full of joy and abundance, then we will attract to ourselves more situations that allow us to experience greater joy and abundance.

The trick is to notice what you are experiencing, and if it is not of your choosing, then by changing your thoughts you change your feelings (and consequently your energetic frequency) and begin to attract things that you would prefer.

The energetic centre through which this process of attraction takes place is the sacral chakra.

The Solar Plexus Chakra

Our next chakra is the solar plexus chakra, located, as you might guess, at our solar plexus, in the upper abdomen. The colour associated with this chakra is yellow, and it relates to our lower back and abdomen, muscles, stomach, pancreas, spleen, liver, gall bladder and autonomic nervous system. This chakra is linked to our sense of personal power, and will. Self-confidence, self-esteem and any lack of these qualities are also associated with this chakra. It is here that we feel fear, or uncertainty, and here that we feel the beginnings of anger if our will is challenged.

This is a powerful centre, and by maintaining plentiful, positive energy within this chakra, we feel strong in ourselves, confident and upbeat about life. This is also the centre associated with the intellect.

The Heart Chakra

Next is the heart chakra, located not at our physical heart, but in the centre of our chest. Our heart chakra is the mid-point of our physical chakra collection, and when we are centred in our heart, we are held in the very centre of our being.

The heart chakra has two colours associated with it: green and pink. Some say that green is because of the colours of the rainbow, often linked with the colours of the chakras. Green is also the colour of balance, and the Heart is a balance-point between the higher and lower chakras.

This chakra is associated with our heart, circulatory system, thymus, lungs, arms and hands, but is better known for its non-physical quality: It is the centre of

Unconditional Love. When we are truly in our heart centre, we are held in the deepest Love, which asks nothing and gives all. This Love is always present within us, and we can access it, and move into its embrace, at any time. When we are centred in our heart, in Unconditional Love, then our lives flow smoothly and joyously. This is the place to Be.

Pink is the colour associated with Unconditional Love, and thus the second colour of the heart chakra is the purest, warmest pink.

The heart chakra is the bridge between the lower and higher chakras. The base, sacral and solar plexus charkas are linked with the physical, our "lower" energies, and the chakras above the heart – throat, brow and crown – are linked with the spiritual, our "higher" energies. The heart is the bridge, the balancing centre between the two, where our lower energies are transmuted into higher frequencies, and our higher frequencies are infused with the lower vibrations, bringing Spirit into our physical experience.

The Throat Chakra

The chakra above the heart is the throat. The colour here is blue, and it is associated with our bronchial tubes, oesophagus, throat, jaw, thyroid and parathyroid glands. The qualities of the throat chakra are communication and nourishment. Communication, or expression out, and nourishment in. This is communication on any level; person to person, and also communication from human to spirit. And nourishment includes nourishment on every level, not only food, but emotional, intellectual and spiritual nourishment as well.

The Brow Chakra

Our next chakra is the brow, or third eye. This is located in the centre of our forehead. Some say its associated colour is indigo, a merging of the blue of the throat with the violet of the crown, and some say it is violet, with the crown chakra being white.

The frequencies of both the brow and crown chakras are high, and the higher in frequency we go, the less clear it becomes to differentiate one energy from another. There is less separation, one merging gradually into the next. As both the brow and crown are linked with "higher vision", and our connection to energies much higher than our own, I feel that the two are closely connected, their colours merging, and at times presenting in one form and at times another.

As our new chakra, the Violet Flame Chakra, sits between these two, we now have three high frequency energy centres within a small physical space, and there will be little separation between them at all.

The brow, or third eye, chakra is associated with our eyes, ears, nose, sinuses and pituitary gland. Its quality, as its name suggests, is "vision", either in terms of creative thought, or of psychic vision - clairvoyance (literally "clear seeing".)

The Crown Chakra

The last of our "normal" chakras is the crown. This is located, as its name suggests, at the top of our head, at our crown. The colour here is white, or some say violet, and it is linked with our brain, central nervous system and pineal gland. Its prime quality, or purpose, is to enable our connection to higher energies, to Spirit.

It is through the crown chakra that we connect up, during meditation, and it is through this chakra that the higher energy flows down to us. When we give healing, or Reiki, it is through the crown that the energy enters our being, before flowing through our heart centre (linking with Unconditional Love), down our arms and then out through our hands. When we receive Channelled guidance, this too enters through our crown chakra. It is our entry and exit portal for our higher spiritual connection.

We have chakras both above our crown and below our base, each with their own colours and qualities, but it is the seven chakras associated with our physical body that are most familiar to us.

Our Chakras as a Whole

These energy centres are all vortices, spinning at all times, and allowing energy to flow both in and out of our being. As the vortex at our base points down, to the earth, so the vortex at our crown points up, to the heavens. For all the intermediate chakras, we have a vortex of energy projecting both forwards and backwards, in the horizontal plane. It is through these that we draw in our experiences and project out our feelings and intentions.

When we are in good health, all the vortices are spinning evenly, neither too rapidly nor too slowly. Our chakras are open, and energy flows freely into and out of our being.

When our energy becomes disturbed, for example through interference on the mental or emotional levels, then our chakras can become closed, or blocked. Our energy no longer flows freely, and poor health, or disease, can result. By clearing the energy within our chakras, and by maintaining a good flow both in and out, health, and increased wellbeing can be restored.

Chapter Two

The Violet Flame Chakra

Although the Violet Flame Chakra is located between the chakras of the brow and crown, here the similarity ends. It is a different creature altogether.

Edwin Courtenay describes it thus:

"The Violet Flame Chakra sits atop the brow, on the highest point of the forehead, and burns with all the colours of the violet light, from deep magenta to pale lilac through violet and purple, with flickers of silver, gold, deep ruby red and opalescent light. It is a living flame and should be seen as such - rather than as a star or orb or vortex of light. It serves to connect us to every manifestation of the Violet Flame found in every dimension that exists between the Divine and ourselves.

"The Violet Flame is found in every Sphere / dimension, where it can be summoned to cleanse and clear negative energy there, from the physical sphere where it can be called upon to transmute toxins and pollutants, to the mental and emotional spheres where it can be called upon to transmute negative thought forms and emotions, as well as the spiritual sphere where it can be called upon to cleanse dark and heavy spiritual energies such as demonic infestation and pollution.

"Although we have always been connected to the Violet Flame of our sphere and (some of us) capable of accessing and channelling the higher energies of the Violet Flame in other Spheres, for most of us there have always been aspects of the Violet Flame which have been beyond our reach - which is why sometimes when we have called upon the Violet Flame it doesn't seem to have worked. Now - through the initiation of the Violet Flame Chakra - this will be a thing of the past, enabling us all to call upon the Flame in every aspect of its manifestation. This, then, is the first new manifestation of the Violet Flame as a new chakra within our energy system, a doorway or window or portal through which the full power of the Flame and its associated wisdom - as well as those Presences connected to it - might be accessed and drawn upon."[1]

---

[1]   Edwin Courtenay's notes from his workshop "St Germain – Harbinger Of The Violet Flame Chakra, The 14th Chakra of the New Galactic Age" on Saturday 23rd November 2013.

This energy, that of the Violet Flame manifesting within us as a Chakra, is powerful indeed, and those of us who have been working with it for some time are continually discovering just how powerful it is.

The Beginning

The first experiences of Awakening the Violet Flame Chakra came during workshops facilitated by Edwin Courtenay in the Autumn of 2013. Edwin is a Channel of many years' experience, and has been working with The Ascended Master Saint-Germain for some time.

I was privileged to attend the second of these workshops, in Surrey at the end of November. The original intention had been a workshop for 50 people, but it soon became clear that more people were drawn to this work. A larger venue was found, and on the day 84 people were present to receive their Awakening. It was a magical occasion.

We experienced the co-creation of a Sacred Space, received the Awakening of the Violet Flame energy within us, focussed on our Violet Flame Chakra, and practised using some of the powerful healing tools that are linked to aspects of the Violet Flame Chakra energy.

Towards the end of the workshop Edwin Channelled Saint-Germain, and we were told that during the day the Violet Flame Chakra of the Earth had also been

Awakened. This is located at Leith Hill, near Dorking, in Surrey, not too far from where we were.

Saint-Germain also told us that the energy of this Earth Chakra would build slowly over the coming months. He asked us to regularly direct energy through our own Violet Flame Chakras towards Leith Hill, to support this process. He said that in time the Chakra would become known internationally as a Sacred Site, and would receive visitors from throughout the globe.

As part of the process of the day, we drew names of the Higher Beings associated with the Violet Flame Chakra. As a Channel for Saint-Germain myself, I was not surprised that the name I drew was: Saint-Germain.

Edwin explained what role we might expect to play within the work of the Violet Flame Chakra, according to the name of the Being we had chosen (or who had chosen us!). To those who had drawn the name of Saint-Germain, he said that we would be involved with spreading this work, sharing information, and taking it forward.

This I have been privileged to do.

Exploring the Tools

My first exploration of the energy of the Violet Flame Chakra came the following day, when I "tried out" some of the healing tools on my Partner, Simon. He is also a powerful healer, therapist and Channel, and as such, both sensitive to higher energies, and a judge of their power.

The tools that I was using were the four "Rescue Flames" that we had been introduced to at the workshop, following the Awakening of our Violet Flame Chakra. These are aspects of the Violet Flame energy which work on specific levels within the recipient. They are for use in times of crisis, hence their name "Rescue" Flames.

As I had practised the previous day, I made the preparation, and directed the Flames, one at a time, towards Simon.

Both he and I could feel the powerful energy of each Flame. They were strong indeed.

My next connection with the Rescue Flames came during the treatment of a client. She was undergoing a course of Setsukido treatments (a transformative therapy combining deep tissue massage and Ki). Intuitively prompted to use these new tools, I made the appropriate connection, and allowed the energy to flow. Again, the process was profoundly powerful, as were the results.

I had been working with energy of differing frequencies for about twenty years – Healing, Reiki, Ki (in Setsukido), Cosmic Energy (a specific frequency) – and had been a Channel for roughly the same length of time. I considered that I was familiar with high frequency vibrations, but the energy of the Rescue Flames was on a different level entirely.

They were powerful, but what I noticed most was that after using them, even for only a brief period – working at that level, very little is needed to effect the necessary change – my own energy took about three days to integrate the consequences of the connection, and I felt I could not connect to any other healing energy within that time. This was new for me, and a further indication of the different nature and degree of power of this new energy.

Chapter Three

Passing on the Awakening

With my Partner, Simon, I have been leading a regular Spiritual Group since early 2010. Initially I Channelled Saint-Germain on a weekly basis, as he assisted us in preparation for the Ascension beginning in 2012. As time went on the meeting frequency and content – and indeed, location as we grew too large for my small flat! – changed, but the Group has continued in one form or another since that time.

As a Teacher, and as a Channel for Saint-Germain, I was keen to pass on the Awakening, and the regular "core" members of our Group seemed the ideal recipients of this process. They were familiar with the energy of Saint-Germain, they could certainly handle the power of these new tools, and it seemed an appropriate gift with which to reward them for their loyalty in following the teachings and guidance of Saint-Germain for so long.

It would also give me the opportunity to practise my new "Awakening" skills on home ground, and among friends.

In December the Awakening was passed on. There were seven people who received this gift, an appropriate number: the number seven forms an integral part of this work.

As my first presentation of the Awakening, it was somewhat stumbling, but with the intention of the Group, and much help from Saint-Germain, the process was accomplished.

Because of time constraints, the process that Edwin had taken us through in a day had to be divided between two of our Group meetings. When we reconvened for the second meeting, we began by sharing our experiences of the tools and energy so far.

I had not shared with the Group my own response to use of the Rescue Flames, but it was interesting to hear from more than one person that they, too, had found them powerful, and after using them had felt quite "knocked out".

We explored a further aspect of the tools associated with the Violet Flame Chakra, I passed on to them Edwin's notes from the original workshop, and their Awakening was complete.

Edwin offers a variety of Attunements / Initiations within his workshops, and always generously shares his notes with those present, so that they may not only benefit themselves from the experiences, but may offer the same experiences to others.

I was therefore privileged to have received his notes on the Awakening, and associated gifts.

Chapter Four

The Process Continues

Having experienced passing on one "Awakening", and being one of those chosen by Saint-Germain to spread this work, I was keen to present my first full day's workshop on the process.

Like Edwin, I discovered that the work was popular; many were drawn to my first offering of this new energy.

Not 84 – thank goodness, the workshop was taking place in my home! – but still more than we had originally anticipated. The increased numbers meant us moving the event from our smaller room to our larger, and even then meant people being squeezed in to every available space. Sixteen in all attended the day at the end of January 2014.

While I am familiar with leading workshops and other presentations, it is usually my own work – created following guidance – that I present. The challenge for me as I prepared for the day was to ensure that the work was presented appropriately, with regard to its spiritual significance, while mentally holding someone else's format and content.

Usually, as the material for a workshop comes together, I "learn" it at the same time. Here, I had to be true to Edwin's subject matter, while presenting it with my own intention and inner connection to the energy. Despite having reviewed and reviewed the content during the preceding days, the early morning of the of the workshop date found me, yet again, going over the order of the day.

It was only then, already within the enclosing energy of the occasion, that things became clear. As they did so, I also received communication from Saint-Germain. He spoke to me of my work with this energy, and affirmed that it would become my own. Therefore, it would be appropriate for me to prepare a manual covering the presentation as **I** did it, which would make it much easier for me to follow, and possibly more effective for those that received it.

This is not to say that no-one else should offer these Awakenings! But in terms of my own progress with it, and my journey with Saint-Germain, it was appropriate for me to "own" it, and present it accordingly.

Of course, such a manual could not be produced for the workshop that day, but feeling that I had been "given permission" to create my own presentation, I was able to relax and allow the full power of the energy to flow.

With a lot of help from Saint-Germain!

The First Workshop

The day was amazing. All who attended were blown away by the energy, their experience, and the potential that they saw. Several of those who attended had already received their Awakening at our Group in December, but wished to experience the process in a more relaxed manner, and spread throughout the day. They all felt that this second "Awakening" was more profound for them than the first.

Preparing for the Second Workshop

Although we had squeezed in 16 for the first full day workshop, there had been more who wished to attend. To accommodate these, and the others who would undoubtedly be drawn to this work, a second date was set for an "Awakening".

For this, I felt able to produce my own manual, and to offer the day in the manner that felt appropriate to me. My previous two offerings of the Awakening had integrated the process within me sufficiently to feel able to run "on trust"; to know that the structure of the day was in place, and to allow the energy to flow freely thereafter.

And so a manual was produced. Not, however, as it could have been, days before the event, with plenty of time to prepare, print and collate…

Although I did begin preparations with (what I felt was) plenty of time, it – as always – took much longer than I anticipated. Once I began to put on paper my own understanding of the Violet Flame Chakra energy, and the process involved in working with it, I found it much more complex than I had thought. I also wished to "tidy up" Edwin's notes; secretarial training several decades previously had imprinted me with the need for order in typed material. If this was going to be my manual, then it would be the best that I could produce.

It is questionable how "best" it was to be printing and binding until 10 o'clock the night before the workshop – and here my long-suffering Partner, Simon, was finally allowed to lend a hand, to my great gratitude – but finished it was, and although I might not have been as rested and centred as I could have been prior to the day, at least the material was fresh in my mind!

The Second Workshop

The second Awakening Day was also a success. (And the manual was duly admired and appreciated, which gratified my Ego somewhat after its determined efforts!)

Fewer numbers, but none the less powerful. Also more comfortable. After the sardine-like experience of the first workshop, we decided to be firm with regard to numbers, and drew the line at the point where we would no longer fit into our more spacious room.

The Awakenings were experienced, the associated tools explored, and, as previously, Guidance and Communication was shared from Saint-Germain. He assured those present that their own individual healing had begun from that day. Of course, many had been consciously upon their individual journey for some time. Some present, though, had been suffering significantly over recent months, working with old negative patterns manifesting in physical symptoms or external situations. It was these particular long-term, soul level, wounds to which he was referring, and the healing of these that he declared would begin from the time of their attendance that day.

And this has been true. For two attendees in particular, that day marked a change in their experiences; symptoms reduced and life changed for them. Others, also, experienced significant changes from the time of that day. His words were true.

Chapter Five

Who is Saint-Germain?

Perhaps it is appropriate here to pause and explore briefly, who is Saint-Germain? Who is this being, possibly a Saint, whose energy is linked with the energy of the Violet Flame Chakra, and whose presence enables and assists the power and transformation of these Awakening Days?

Saint-Germain is not a Saint. The name we use comes from his most recent incarnation, as a French Count in the 18th Century. He was, then, Le Comte de Saint-Germain. In that life he was also known as The Wonder Man of Europe. Even then, he had "magical" abilities; some say he lived to be 100 years old, and held the Elixir of Life. He was an accomplished musician and artist, and moved in high society. It has also been said that he would be seen in different places - different countries, even - at around the same time. In the days before supersonic travel, was this the use of some secret power?

He was an alchemist, that is for sure. His knowledge of the elements, and alchemical processes is widely recognised, as is his skill in this regard. He may well have been one of the many engaged in the attempt to transmute base metal into gold.

He may have succeeded.

Saint-Germain's Journey

But what of his greater journey, his spiritual progression? There are many sources of information about his many lives, and you are welcome to explore them all. I would recommend one book by Edwin Courtenay: "Reflections, The Masters Remember", in which several Ascended Masters review their various incarnations, from the perspective of more recent times. The section on Saint-Germain is worth reading.

As a Channel for him, I tried deliberately, in the beginning, to research as little as possible. I did not want any conscious knowledge I might have to interfere with, or to influence, the communications that came through from him. But information is out there, and I could not avoid, through different synchronicities and discoveries, learning something about the earlier story of the Being who now works with me - to my great gratitude and undying privilege, I might add.

So, my potted history of The Ascended Master, Saint-Germain – supported by intuition and some prompting from The Man himself -, goes like this:

He was, indeed, an 18th Century French Count, skilled in music and many other arts; an alchemist and one who lived in awareness of realms beyond the physical.

In an earlier incarnation he was Francis Bacon, the true author of many of Shakespeare's plays.

In an even earlier incarnation he was Merlin, the Magician at King Arthur's Court. The term "Merlin" is said to mean "Teacher", and this he may have been, teaching and guiding Arthur through his life journey. But "the" Merlin, as we know him, I feel was someone special, and carried a slightly different interpretation of the name.

This same Soul also lived in the time of Jesus, in the person of Joseph of Arimathea. Much is written about this character, but my feeling is that – although that time is so buried in the past as to be not easily accessible – "Joseph" was linked to Jesus, and played an important role in his journey, and the story we are familiar with today.

A story we may be less familiar, or initially comfortable, with, is the story that Joseph travelled to England with Mary Magdalene, the mother of Jesus' children. Here, too, he played an important role in the Journey as a whole.

This Energy, this Essence, has had many other lives; as with us all: some significant in terms of planetary and humanity's evolution, and some not, allowing the soul to grow and develop all the attributes it needs to fulfil its part in the Divine Whole.

An Incarnation in Atlantis

The Being that we know as Saint-Germain has one other life that we should take note of: one in Atlantean times.

Here, again, much is written, and much conflicts, but here, as in all things, we should trust our own inner guidance and determine what is our own truth. There are differing opinions of "Atlantis", and different time-periods in history when it is meant to have existed. But Saint-Germain said to us some months ago, in our regular Group, that Atlantis was not so much a time or geographical location, as a frequency. A vibration of energy. When people speak of returning to the time of Atlantis, or that we are – in current times – re-connecting with Atlantis – it is the *frequency* of Atlantis with which we link, not a place or a moment in time past.

In Atlantis, wherever and whenever it may have been experienced, there was great knowledge of all things spiritual, and non-physical. The healing techniques, and use of crystals and sound were far beyond any processes or knowledge that we have today. (Although we are rapidly catching up; the changes since the Winter Solstice in 2012 have seen to that!)

Life was very different; great harmony between all, and, it is said, beautiful colours in plants and surroundings.

Through Saint-Germain's guidance with us at our Group we have all been privileged to connect to the energy of Atlantean times, and I have also been fortunate to return to that frequency during some past life memories of my own. It is a truly wonderful environment, and if we are moving towards returning to that way of living, then Praise Be!

Saint-Germain, or the Soul we know by that name, lived in Atlantean times. He was a Priest in the Healing Temple there, and it was he who led the exploration of a new system of healing which had been given – through Divine Guidance – to the Temple's High Priest. This High Priest instructed his pupil in the new modality, but it was Saint-Germain who explored it. It was

Saint-Germain who tried the processes, noted the experiences, instructed his own students and noted the results and their experiences, learning and adapting all the time.

It is appropriate, then, that he is working with us as we explore the energy and properties of the tools associated with the Violet Flame Chakra.

This Ancient Atlantean healing system has continued on down through the ages, sometimes coming to the fore sometimes falling away, but always present, and always, to some degree, under the overwatching presence of the energy we know as Saint-Germain. In its current form, this healing system is recognised throughout the world, many people practise it and many have benefitted from its power. We know it as Reiki.

Ascended Masters

One further note of explanation, perhaps, is valid. Saint-Germain is referred to as an Ascended Master. What is this?

An Ascended Master is a High Soul, that once (or more than once) was incarnate in physical form. On a Soul Level, they have Ascended - risen in frequency until they become Light – but they choose to remain associated with those on the Earth plane, and to help them with their journey.

There are many Ascended Masters, the most familiar being Jesus, The Buddha, and Mother Mary. In subtle energetic terms these Beings have a similar frequency to that of Archangels, indeed, Archangel Michael is both an Archangel (as the name suggests) and an Ascended Master. Like all high frequency, non-physical Beings, Ascended Masters can be called upon for assistance at any time. Always, in the moment of asking, help is given; we must remember that. Archangels and Ascended Masters often work closely together.

We are privileged to have the support of such glorious Beings assisting us on our Human journey, and I feel very privileged to be a Channel for The Ascended Master, Saint-Germain.

Chapter Six

What is Channelling?

And a further question, perhaps: What is Channelling?

In simple terms, this is the allowing, by a physical being, of the merging of a Higher Energy with theirs. During this process the physical being is able to convey (Channel) information from the Higher Being to others, thus acting as a conduit, or Channel, for the information and energy.

There are varying degrees of Channelling. For me, "full" Channelling is when my energy merges with another, higher frequency, such as Saint-Germain. I feel his energy, and become aware of words or concepts which I then, vocally, convey. During this process, I remain conscious, present, and aware of the information being communicated.

Some Channels move into a state of meditation, or trance, and have no knowledge or memory of what was said or what took place during the Channelling. In this form of Channelling, the physical form of the Channel often changes; the voice becoming deeper, or taking on another intonation or accent. The facial expression can also change, and the physical body move in a different way, or change its habitual position.

These changes happen because the incoming Energy "overlays" its frequency, and characteristics, on the human Channel. It is not uncomfortable, or unpleasant, and indeed, the Channel often has no memory of this benevolent "invasion".

This form of Channelling used to be the norm until the last twenty years or so, and some Channels today still work in this way.

I have always remained aware of what has been taking place during Channelling, and as a result have been privileged to "hear" much wisdom and inspiration during my Channelling career.

I did not set out to be a Channel; indeed before my first Channelling experience I knew nothing about it, and did not know that such a process even existed! Such is the magic of Spirit.

My First Channelling

My introduction to being a Channel came in the most unlikely way. I was alone, at a friend's house, having made the mile walk there to feed their goldfish while they were on holiday. The fish being duly nourished, I sat for a few minutes, before setting off on the journey back.

As I sat, I became aware of a strange sensation in the centre of my chest, as if there was "something" there. I was very new to Spiritual work (in this lifetime) yet not unduly worried at the sensation. I felt it was OK, and so I did nothing to dispel it. I closed my eyes, interested to see what, if anything, would happen next.

What did happen next was that I felt my arms begin to lift by my sides, gradually rising until my hands were above my head, elbows bent and palms upwards. Again, the sensation was not unpleasant, and I remained with it, interested in the new experience.

The sensations increased, and I began to feel that I was almost buzzing with energy. I could feel my hands very strongly, and knew exactly where they were; about six inches above my head.

After a minute or two, curiosity got the better of me, and I opened my eyes to see what my hands looked like, with all this energy buzzing through them.

To my utter amazement, although I could *feel* distinctly where they were, when I looked, I saw that they were several inches lower than where I could feel them. For a few moments I continued looking, hardly able to believe my eyes. My visual information told me that my hands were about level with my head. But my awareness of them, as a result of the buzzing energy, was that they were several inches higher. It was a strange situation!

After a short time the energy, both within my hands and within my chest, began to disperse, and I felt able to lower my hands. My visual and sensual information systems re-united once more: my hands felt as if they were where I could see they were, and the whole process drew to a close.

I sat for a few minutes longer, wanting to process this experience a little before venturing out into the hustle and bustle of town streets on my walk home.

When I felt ready, I set off, and as I made my way back, I felt as if there was an echo of a much taller "me" around me as I walked.

The Experience Explained

I attended a regular Spiritual Development Group at that time, and when we next met I couldn't wait to ask the lady who led the Group what might have been happening during my strange experience.

Her reply was very matter-of-fact. "Oh, you were Channelling Ptah". This didn't help me much; it generated more questions: "What's Channelling, and who's Pa?"

She explained about Channelling and told me that Ptah (Ptahotep, to give him his full title) was an ancient Egyptian. She herself was an accomplished Channel, and Ptah was one of the many Energies she worked with. His Egyptian connection explained the "hands above the head" pose - often shown in Egyptian images. She suggested that I tried Channelling him again, that evening within the Group, and this I did.

Channelling Ptah

This was in 1992, and for the next 18 months or so Ptah was a regular "visitor". My indication that he was around was a change in energy within the environment, and the slow rising of my hands into what became referred to as "Ptah's position".

As I became familiar with his energy, and the Channelling process, the sessions would last longer, sometimes up to an hour, and I was able to "hold" my hands in that position for that time. It was no strain to do so, and I felt no stiffness in the muscles afterwards.

On the occasions that I doubted the validity of the whole experience, I would hold my hands up there without Ptah's assisting presence, and within a matter of moments realise that it would be impossible to maintain that pose for any length of time under my own steam.

It was a privilege to Channel Ptah, and through his assistance I learnt a great deal. He would "visit" most frequently when I was in the company of the friend whose house had been the first venue for our connection. John, a good friend and valued fellow traveller on my spiritual journey, had many questions for Ptah, on a wide range of subjects, and Ptah shared much knowledge with us.

His regular presence also enabled me to become familiar with Channelling, and to allow my energy to adjust to the regular connection with another, higher, frequency.

Channelling Other Beings

Many years later Channelling "returned" to me again, following my Attunement to Reiki Level Two, and I would regularly Channel un-named Higher Beings during Guidance sessions for my clients.

I was also privileged to become a Channel for a Group Consciousness: an energy of a specific frequency known as the Cosmic Energies. This was a vibration new to the Earth and at that time – 2004 – was the highest frequency connecting to our planet. Their Cosmic Energies story is amazing in itself, but must be set aside here to focus on Saint-Germain.

Saint-Germain Approaches

I had heard of Saint-Germain; I knew the name, and that he was associated with the I Am teachings, and also something called the Violet Flame, but there my knowledge ended. I had had no connection with him (that I was aware of!) and had plenty of other energies and new healing techniques - and my own inner Spiritual journey – to keep me busy without seeking out more Beings to connect with!

I had been working with some other Ascended Masters – as seems the way with my journey, these Beings approach me, rather than the other way around – Melchisadek, El Morya and Archangel Michael in particular. They often came forward during healing treatments for my clients.

During the Autumn of 2009 I gradually became aware of another Presence during treatments. Always in the background, but often there. Their energy felt comfortable, and I felt no need to explore further.

I knew they would come forward if and when they wanted to.

And they did! One Thursday morning in January 2010, during the time it took to make the bed, I "knew" that the Presence had been Saint-Germain, and that he wanted me to hold a regular weekly group, where I would Channel him, as he prepared us for the Ascension, anticipated in December 2012.

Just like that.

I'd never worked with him before. I'd never Channelled him before. But that was his plan, and I trusted it would happen.

Chapter Seven

The Ascension Group Begins

I emailed out to those that I felt would be open to it, and willing to "explore" with me. I received a positive response, so it appeared that he knew what he was doing, and that the occasion would take place.

On the night, 15 people squeezed themselves into my small flat. I had not been prompted to Channel him before the appointed evening, and I trusted that it would all unfold as it should.

When we were all gathered, I settled myself into my "Teacher's" chair, opened my arms into receiving mode, and, after a breath or two, began to Channel the energy of The Ascended Master, Saint-Germain.

This was the beginning of an amazing and greatly privileged journey. It has been an honour to receive his energy, and to allow it to be experienced by others.

I have Channelled Saint-Germain to our regular Group; I have Channelled him during whole day workshops, where the healing and transformation that have taken place have been magical. I have Channelled him for individuals, enabling healing on many levels in addition to the words of guidance that he brings.

I have passed on his words in person, by phone, and through email. He also, now, regularly "Tweets", through messages – which hold his energy – Channelled through me. It is a joy, and a privilege to partner him in this way. I feel truly blessed.

From those gathered on that first evening in my flat some were never drawn to receive more than they gained on that first occasion. Others returned, week after week, for more of his energy, and more of his wisdom. By the Autumn of that year our numbers had grown; a new venue was found, and the Group continued to expand.

Preparing for Ascension

During our time at the Group Saint-Germain's teaching covered many topics. In the early days people would ask questions, often relating to how things would be following the shift in energy that we anticipated in 2012. He continually reassured us, encouraging us to make our own progress towards our individual Ascension.

In addition to information, relating to the coming change and other matters, we were often privileged to assist in energetic processes, providing a link between the physical plane and the higher frequency energies that were working to enable the Ascension transition on other levels. On many occasions Saint-Germain expressed thanks on behalf of himself and other Energies, for our part in enabling an anchoring of energy within the Earth.

He led us, too, in exercises intended to raise our own frequency, and the levels we reached during those expansions was at times profound.

Within his communications with us Saint-Germain had (and still has!) recurring themes. He will often encourage us to "Look up, Beloveds; Look up, for that is the direction in which you will then move." Joy is another popular message of his, reminding us that we hold Joy within us at all times, and that it is a choice whether we connect with it or not.

He reminds us that we are all "Glorious Beings of Light" and encourages us to recognise that, and honour ourselves for it. He frequently describes us as "Magnificent".

I should say, here, that there is nothing special about our little group, and that we are all, every one of us – including you, as you read this book – "Glorious Beings of Light" and "Magnificent".

Another theme which Saint-Germain drew on regularly, as December 2012 approached, was that we should "Step into our Mastery". He repeated that the time was coming when we would no longer need to seek guidance from outside ourselves, applying to Beings that we perceived to be greater than ourselves before taking action or making decisions. Time and again he encouraged us to trust our own inner wisdom, to believe in ourselves and our own capabilities, and told us that we were capable of far more than we allowed ourselves to experience. As we believed, so were we limited. He encouraged us to revise those perceived limitations, and to move beyond them.

With the change in energy expected around December 2012, there would be a shift into greater power. It would no longer be appropriate for us to question, to hesitate, to seek approval or affirmation from Beings – however apparently high – outside ourselves. We were Masters, and as such, we should own our Mastery, and act accordingly.

At times he could be quite insistent on this. For our own good, as he would assure us; he always spoke in the highest love and light.

And sometimes with great humour! On one occasion, as a means of lightening the atmosphere after a particularly intense energy-awareness process, he invited us to imagine that we were each holding a brightly coloured balloon. He then suggested that we "float" these balloons across the room, to others present. As the balloons, in their different bright colours, began to be batted to and fro he encouraged us to become light, and bright, and to move with them. He has laughingly referred back to our "balloons" since that time.

There were more serious experiences, too; clearing old energy, holding the space to enable a greater concentration of energy to reach the earth than had been possible before, and, often, a "radiating out" of Light, as a Beacon to those that sought it.

Much of Saint-Germain's teaching was in preparation for the Solstice Shift, and enabling change that would assist that Shift in coming into being. Once the time had passed, his connection with us changed.

After the Winter Solstice

Saint-Germain was present on the first couple of occasions in January 2013, assisting us to settle in to the new energies. But then his messages changed. Again, he encouraged us to "step into our Mastery", to "own our power". He said that, as with a young child, it does not serve to carry that child. Once it is ready, it is appropriate that it should stand on its own two feet, and learn to walk. Continuing to carry it does not serve the child, nor indeed the parent. He therefore, in the highest love and light, was going to step back, and allow us to learn to walk.

As with a caring parent, he would always be nearby, but we should trust ourselves to take the step into our own Mastery, and begin to recognise our own inherent wisdom. Therefore, his presence would be less apparent within our meetings, and we would be left to guide ourselves.

This we did, and continued to have an interesting, shared, journey through the next few months of 2013. Occasionally Saint-Germain would come forward, and communicate with us, and we came to treasure these occasions, and value them more highly.

And then came the Violet Flame Chakra.

Following my attendance at Edwin's workshop in November, I was guided by Saint-Germain to Awaken the Violet Flame Chakras of the regular members of our Group. He was keen, not only to spread this new energy, but, more importantly, to reward those who had worked so faithfully with him and enabled and assisted so much as we moved towards 2012.

It was very much a gift from him to "his" Group.

With our Chakras Awakened, and a Living Violet Flame burning within our meeting space, our Group meetings once again took on a new form. As we learnt to work with these new energies, we had many experiences to share as we gathered together. The more we worked with these new tools, the more we came to realise just how powerful and transformative they were.

The Violet Flame

Perhaps it is appropriate here to mention something of the "original" Violet Flame, that energy that has been used, in one form or another, for centuries.

The Violet Flame itself is a powerful tool of transmutation. It can be invoked by anyone – no Awakening is needed to enable its use. It will transmute any negative energies into a higher form – positive energy – thus preventing the attachment to or contamination of other beings or situations by the negative energy. During any healing process, particularly when old, negative energy is consciously released, it is wise to invoke the Violet Flame to cleanse and clear the space as the work is done.

Saint-Germain has long been associated with the Violet Flame. The dictionary definition of "transmute" (to change the form of) also includes reference to the alchemical process of transmuting base metal into gold. As Saint-Germain (in his incarnation of that name) was known to be an alchemist - and I suspect that skill was familiar to him in earlier lives as well - it is appropriate that he should be associated with a powerful healing tool that echoes an alchemical process.

Chapter Eight

The Violet Flame Chakra – New Processes Evolve

Those of us who had been "Awakened" continued to work with the energy of the Violet Flame Chakra, and its associated tools. As with many healing modalities in the times since December 2012, things were changing. New ideas came, and new processes were explored.

Saint-Germain had said to us at our regular Group, on more than one occasion, that in these times, with regard to healing, whatever we could think of doing, we could do. If an idea came, we could pursue it; however "off the wall" and crazy it might be. We could trust that it would be safe, and that all would be well.

During a dream, I received guidance to combine the Rescue Flames with a process from Setsukido, the deep tissue massage therapy that I practice and teach. The Setsukido umbrella extends way beyond straightforward body work, incorporating Ki, the meridian system, the clearing and release of old emotional patterns, and past life connection.

Within Setsukido there is a technique where we work with the Sacrum – or "Sacred Sacrum" – the large bone at the base of the spine. Within the sacrum are four pairs of "holes", and these can be used as energetic gateways, through which to access past lives.

I was guided to combine the use of the gateways with the four Rescue Flames, channelling each Flame into a pair of "gateways", and thus clearing and transmuting past lives, the present, and also our pathway into the future.

This sounded powerful, and profound, but intuitively felt right, and so I explored the process with my Partner, Simon. We practised it on each other, giving feedback, and were very aware of the difference in energy from gateway to gateway, and the change that took place within the experience.

I was a little hesitant about adding to the Rescue Flames. At our "Awakening" nothing had been said – either by Edwin, or Channelled from Saint-Germain – about exploring and expanding around the initial tools we were given. Was it right to be meddling with these gifts? But it felt comfortable, and so I trusted that it was appropriate.

The Divine, of course, knew exactly what it was doing.

Liz's Gifts

One of those attending the first full day's Awakening workshop that I offered was a beautiful Soul called Liz. Liz had been working with Saint-Germain for many years, and using the Violet Flame in its original form. A few Christmases ago she presented me with a beautiful "Co-Creation", as she termed it: a silk painted and embroidered wall hanging of an image of the Violet Flame with a crystal obelisk in the centre. She had been guided by Saint-Germain to make it as a gift for me, and I am honoured to have it within my healing space and at my workshops.

As I myself had done, when the time came to choose (or be chosen by) a Higher Being associated with the Violet Flame Chakra, Liz also drew Saint-Germain. Having done so, it became clear that she, too, would be involved in spreading the Violet Flame Chakra teachings further.

She embraced this, and applied it literally: Enabling a Violet Flame Chakra Awakening within a spiritual friend of hers in Australia.

"Distant" Awakenings

We had not been told that Awakenings could be carried out over distance, but I had already enabled this, with a powerful Reiki Master-student of mine. Matthew had been an integral part of the early Ascension Group gatherings, and continued to work closely with Saint-Germain. On hearing about this latest work, he said that he felt he should receive this Awakening, and, through our shared intention, this was accomplished (with a little help from Saint-Germain). Matthew was abroad at the time.

When Liz mentioned that she had carried out a "distant" Awakening, I was able to reassure her that I had done the same, and it appeared to be effective.

It is worth saying here that, although this can be done over distance, as has been demonstrated, it is more appropriate, and generally more beneficial to all parties, if it can be carried out "in person". Both Matthew and Mesheril, Liz's friend in Australia, are exceptional beings, and it may not be appropriate in other situations.

More Rescue Flames

Around the time that I was guided to work with the Sacral Gateways, Liz told me that she and Mesheril had been "given" more Rescue Flames. I did question for a moment the validity of this – should we be tampering with the tools we have? – but was certain in my own guidance with regard to combing the first four Flames with the Sacrum, and this seemed a further expansion of the work.

Liz emailed me information on the new Flames. These, too, had been a co-creation, between her and Mesheril: each had become aware of new flames - their colour, associated Presence and purpose – and through exploration, collaboration, trust and intuition, was able to provide confirmation for the other. Through this process a total of seven more Rescue Flames was added.

Chapter Nine

The Violet Flame Chakra Stage Two

Having offered my first full day's "Awakening" experience in January, and also in March for the overflow, and more, I set a further date in May to offer Awakenings again. As with the earlier dates, the event soon filled up with potential students. People who had not been able to join us on the earlier dates, people who had only just heard of this work, and one who had attended previously and planned to bring a group of spiritual friends to share the experience. It was happening!

And then, some weeks before the event, one by one, people began to withdraw. Diary dates clashed; a pet was due to give birth; and the group of spiritual friends had a more urgent focus for their collective energy.

As the potential numbers began to dwindle, I began to feel that there was clearly another Plan for the day. It still felt appropriate to offer something in relation to the Violet Flame Chakra, but perhaps not another Awakening.

I had received guidance about further work with the Flames in the Setsukido process, and I knew Liz had received more Flames – perhaps other "Awakened Ones" also had information and experiences to share? This work was new; there was no text book to which we could refer. The only information we had was what we were discovering for ourselves. It felt appropriate to invite those who had been working with the Flames to come and share their experiences and pool their knowledge.

This I did, and the response indicated that this was, indeed, the Higher Plan for the day.

In order to plan the day, I had asked those attending if they had any specific information to share. Although they had experiences, only Liz and I had received new information and processes. She agreed to share the day with me, and to pass on the details of the new Flames she had received.

A couple of days before the workshop, Liz and Mesheril, again, received yet more Flames! Four new ones were added to the collection. Because they were so new, Liz had not had time to explore them, or name them, and her feeling was that we would all work together with them during the day, and between us determine their finer use and purpose.

The schedule for the day included Channelling from Saint-Germain, some sharing of experiences, and then a brief introduction to the Setsukido / Sacrum process, incorporating the Flames. Because the process was profound, it was not appropriate to use it fully within the group situation, but as many of the students were not familiar with body work, it was important that they were able to connect to the energy gateways, and this we practised within the space.

Then it was time for Liz to introduce her new Flames.

The New Flames

She began with the seven that had come through some time ago, and which she had had the opportunity to use and to explore. She shared with us how each one had come about, and the effects the Flames had had when she and Mesheril employed them.

Each Rescue Flame has a colour (some quite magnificent) and an associated Presence (Higher Being) and a specific purpose. The addition of further Flames beyond the initial four enables us to work with greater precision, selecting and directing the perfect Flame for the matter in hand.

We then had the opportunity to experience the new Flames for ourselves, pairing up, and, through Liz's guidance, allowing one Flame through at a time. They were the most amazing energies, and clearly something new and very special.

After lunch she introduced us to the newest, four, Flames. As she read the brief information held so far on each one, we contributed our thoughts and insights, adding to or confirming what had already been received.

We then had the privilege of exploring these Flames. Again, in pairs, Liz led us in connecting to these new vibrations, and each of us experienced different responses to the new energies being introduced. All of them were powerful, and yet subtle, and it was such a privilege to be in the forefront of the unfolding of this amazing new work.

Liz then showed us a (physical!) gift she had received a few days earlier. Some years ago she had received her Attunement to Reiki Level One in unusual circumstances. The Attunement had been a gift. Recently, Liz had given a gift – the Awakening – to the Reiki Master who had Attuned her.

In exchange, although the Awakening was an exchange-gift, the lady sent Liz a little crystal Angel. The stone was translucent, and yet displayed flashes of many colours within its multi-facets.

Liz passed the crystal angel round, and each one of us who held it "saw" something different within it, and connected to a different energy. Some saw the red-gold of a Rescue Flame; some orange, reflecting the sacral energy; more than one of us recognised the energy of the Divine Feminine within it, and of Mother Mary. When one student held it, in full awareness of the energy of Mother Mary, the angel gradually became more and more blue.

Clearly, there were many energies within it, and as we passed it around the twelve of us assembled, we each connected, saw what was appropriate for us to see, and unknowingly added some of our own energy to the crystal being.

A Gift from Saint-Germain

When it was returned to Liz, our feeling was that it held many different energies, and aspects of many of the Rescue Flames. A sudden inspiration made me speak, but before I could express, in my own words, the understanding just given to me, I had to pause and allow the energy of Saint-Germain to speak to us of the energy we had shared together.

This crystal, he said, was a manifestation of "The One Which Holds All". The crystal Angel was One, and yet within it it held All the energies. Not only all the energies of the many Rescue Flames, but the Energy of All.

This was not a Flame, but an Essence, and this Essence was the Essence of The One, Which Holds All.

It has been said that everything holds within it the energy of The Whole. Everything is part of the The Whole, as we are part of The Whole.

But this crystal was a manifestation – within this Dimension – of the Essence which had condensed into such density as to be One, a single point; one frequency only. One, and yet within that One was The All. Everything, in every frequency in every dimension; all held within the Essence of this One that we held, physically, within our space.

It was a profound time. The energy of The Ascended Master Saint-Germain, as he shared this knowledge, and this Gift, with us, was powerful and fully present. It was a time of great energy, insight, unfoldment and understanding. We were all aware of the depth and power of this expression, and of this wondrous Gift.

Within Saint-Germain's expression, and the presence of the crystal into which we had each linked our energy, we all received Attunement to the Essence of The One Which Holds All. We were told that this was a Gift to us, for our work in exploring and refining the energies of the new Rescue Flames. For the time being, it was a gift for us to hold. To use the Essence if we felt guided to do so, but not, at this time, to pass the Attunement to the Essence on. That may come in time, but for now, it was our Gift, in exchange for our work done.

We all felt humbled, honoured and deeply blessed.

Liz later determined that both Mesheril and Edwin had received the Essence Attunement at the time that we did. Without their help, of course, this day and this experience would not have come into being.

Chapter Ten

Personal Transformation

It is not unusual, following any workshop or connection to high frequencies, to undergo a shift in our personal energy as a result. It is certainly not unusual for me. The shift that took place following this workshop, and high level energy connection, however, was the most profound I have experienced.

It included the connection to and relinquishing of a long-held past life bond, one which had influenced my actions and behaviour in this life, and, indeed, in many intervening lives. The releasing of this energy enabled the letting go of an emotional thread which had been present – sometimes in the background and sometimes very evident – for half a century. The release of it was deep, powerful (not particularly comfortable) and moving. When the transition was over, and it took a number of days to fully integrate, I felt, literally, like a new being.

I was not alone in the deep shifts that were experienced following our sharing. For many of those present, it was a time of great transition and new growth. We had been blessed indeed.

Sharing Insights

As the work was so new, and we had only been together for a few hours during the Saturday workshop – time enough to experience the change, but not sufficient to recognise the full implications of it – the insights and understandings came thick and fast over the next couple of days as things shifted and fell into place.

The electronic pathways hummed with our new information, as we became inspired, "saw the light" and hurried to share our insights with our fellow travellers. Although it was a Sunday (normally a "desk-free" day for me) I was keen to share my insights with others, and on opening my emails found a collection of other information waiting to be passed on. As the hub of the organisation, initially all messages passed through me, and it was a couple of hours before the words, thoughts and wonderful new energy had all been distributed.

We had one of our regular Group meetings the following Thursday, and as, of the 12 attending that evening, six had been at the recent workshop (and all but one of the Group had received the initial Awakening) it is not surprising that the primary subject for the occasion was our latest work. Those that had attended shared how profound the experience had been for them, and, for many, how different they felt as a result. It seems that I was not alone in feeling that I was a new being, or at least, working from a new level.

This Book

The inspiration for this book came following the workshop. One student had brought a book with her, intending to offer it to anyone who felt drawn to it. She had not done so, and I found it lying beside her chair when tidying the room. The content of the book was interesting, and I found some useful new ideas within it, but the main message – for me – was the structure of the book itself. Its size was manageable, and suddenly I felt that I could write such a book. It was, as they say, "do-able".

I had been planning to write a book, on a different Spiritual topic, for some weeks. Indeed, the plan tracked back some 10 years, from the inception of the work! But I had not been able to begin.

Suddenly, I felt I was ready. That I could write, just allow the words to flow, get them down on paper, and facilitate the further spreading of this glorious work. A holiday approached, a couple of weeks ahead, and, having counted the number of words it was necessary to write, and knowing (from the production of a recent magazine article; the Divine works well!) how many words there were to an A4 page, and, from my Channelled Answers from Saint-Germain, how long it took to produce a page – I calculated I had time to write it before our trip away!

Suddenly it all felt possible; it all fell into place. The energy was certainly high, there was a glorious wave of it rushing along at that time, and if I caught it, and rode it, then the work would be easy.

By the end of the week I had begun. My first 3,500 words had been written, and the book was happening.

It has been guided, clearly. Not only in the inception of it, but through each stage. I have definitively been shown each step; I had no plan when I began, but each section has been revealed as I approached it. We are never in need of more vision than the next forward step. Though our human mind and Ego-Self may wish for more!

Another blessing was that the work could include some Channelled contribution from Saint-Germain – making the writing even easier. Here my role is simply to type the words that I receive.

It is my privilege to do this now, and to invite you to experience, for yourself, the loving energy of The Ascended Master, Saint-Germain.

Read, and enjoy.

Chapter Eleven

(CHANNELLING FROM SAINT-GERMAIN)

Greeting

"Most Beloved One, I come to you through the medium of these written words, but do not feel that our connection is limited to such. Open your awareness to my energy, and you will feel my Presence with you as you read.

Enjoy, Dear One, this is a gift for you.

While we are within this space, take some time to still yourself, to quieten the mind. This may seem to be a contradiction in terms, as you are utilising your mind as you read. But your mind may be still as it receives these words, aware only of that which is written, and gently relinquishing all other thoughts.

Be Still, Beloved, Be Still. Let your breathing slow, your body rest and your mind find Peace. And in that Peace, know the tranquillity which dwells within the heart of your Being. That Peace which is always present, always there, waiting only for you to turn your attention to it once more, so that it can find you, embrace you, hold you, as you hold it within you.

Know Peace, Beloved, and know that All Is Well.

The Energy of the Violet Flame

This is an energy which goes back to beyond time. In Ancient Days there were many Energies upon the Earth, indeed, there were many Energies within the Earth. The minerals, crystals, that you know today are manifestations of those energies, each crystal carrying a different frequency, each manifestation holding a different Energy within it. All linked, all working together in harmony, weaving multi-stranded threads to bring together the Presence that is your Earth.

In early times, Beloveds, matter had not condensified (sic) sufficiently to manifest in solid form. The Earth, and energies around it remained, initially, in subtle form. But over time, Dear Ones, as is still the case today, energies, if held, focussed, allowed to resonate sufficiently, con-dense. Become more gross in their manifestation, and, in time, present in physicality.

Thus, your Earth formed. Still, holding around her, and within her, many energies which remained non-physical in their subtle manifestation.

"Time" if we may use that term, for the progressing evolution of The Whole, continued. Much is written in other posts on the progressive journey of your sphere, and this is not the place for such instruction.

Our journey here concerns the energy, the vibration, the frequency of The Violet Flame.

A Sacred Flame

This began, Most Beloveds, as a Sacred Flame. Used in ceremonies and in temples in the earliest times. A Living Flame which burned to hold the energy of those present and of the energy with which they chose to connect. An anchor, if you will, between those higher energies and the living vessels who worked with them.

Its essence was known only to a few. Those souls who understood its power, and its manifestation. Only those who recognised the power behind it were entrusted with its use. It was sacred, blessed, indeed.

In my incarnation of a life within a Temple in Atlantis (and as has been said, seek not this energy within a time or place, but in a frequency, Beloveds, for it is there that it resides) I first encountered the energy of The Violet Flame.

It burned within our Temple, in an inner sanctuary, held for such a frequency. My first connection with it was profound. It was through an Awakening, an initiation, that I first received its energy within my Being. My Soul was touched, trembled at the power and the majesty of this great energy, and I was humbled that I should be considered worthy to receive it, and to direct its force.

For those perhaps less versed in ways of subtle energy, I should explain that, although it was – and is – a Living Flame, it was not visible through physical eyes. The "burning" within our Temple was not seen, but it was felt, the presence of this powerful energy, resonating through the building, and our hearts.

My Connection with the Violet Flame

My first connection with this living power, as a young Priest, touched me deeply. I was blessed with a Seeing of my own path, stretching ahead through time, and carrying within it a strong connection to the energy of this living Flame. I knew then that my path, and that of the energy of the Violet Flame were interwoven, its energy, and my own, dancing through time, first one and then the other coming to the fore, working together always for harmony and the greater good.

Having been touched by the Flame, I was keen to connect with it again and again. When my duties allowed, I would be found within the Sanctuary of the Flame, praying, connecting, experiencing. Through these connections my Soul expanded and my awareness and experience of subtle frequencies were magnified.

It was this dedication to the path of the Violet Flame which led our High Priest-Master to entrust me with the exploration and instigation of the healing practise currently known as Reiki. This was another Gift, which I was honoured to receive. It was a joy to share it with my students then, and it has been a joy to watch its resurgence in more recent times, and to recognise how many practise it and how many more benefit from such practise.

The energy of the Violet Flame continued to be used within Temples and by those who understood its power for some time.

Atlantis Falls

Again, there are many writings of the fall of Atlantis – which, in truth, was, you will now understand, a fall in frequency. Many teachings went "underground"; they were kept hidden, sacred; secret. Some teachings were lost, some hidden in deep treasures only now being rediscovered, as the energy and frequency of human-kind returns towards its zenith, and beyond.

Negative energies – borne from thought, as all creations are, spread. As the frequency of the civilisation fell, these negative energies became more prevalent, lowering the frequency still further.

Now my days within the Sanctuary of the Violet Flame could be no more. Our Temples were destroyed, our sacred energies abused.

But the Living Flame still burned within our hearts. I, and others devoted to our path, carried within our Being the energy of that Living Flame. We invoked it still, to centre us, transform us and inspire.

As our energy became defiled by the negativity surrounding us, we sought a means of cleansing, clearing those energies that attached to us. We had rituals of purification, and these we employed, but the energy we thus released had to go somewhere, and we were concerned to add it to the already growing negative accumulation.

Guidance was sought, and was given. We were instructed to invoke The Violet Flame. Not, as we had known it previously, in its aspect of inspiring and uplifting. But in a new form, an energy of transmutation. Clearing and cleansing, purifying and dissolving, and then – transforming. Changing that which had been negative into that which was positive. Transforming the old into the new. Moving that which was, into something better. Transmuting: changing the form of. Re-forming the energy of negativity into something powerful with the energy of positivity.

The Violet Flame of Transmutation had been born.

Chapter Twelve

(CHANNELLING FROM SAINT-GERMAIN)

The Violet Flame of Transmutation

We used it frequently, transmuting energy within ourselves and in our surroundings. We learnt to "send" this energy, visualising its arrival and its power in people and locations far removed. And with each using of it, it became more embedded within our consciousness, aligning us to its own energy, and enabling us to call upon it easily and swiftly, and to great effect.

Time passed, Beloveds, and the use of the energy of the Violet Flame continued, the employment of it limited, still, to those who had studied Ancient Lore, and whose frequency was appropriate to this vibrational tool.

The knowledge of its power and its use remained sacred; secret, not revealed to the masses who might not understand its majesty.

Despite its hidden use, the numbers who could wield its power were many, and many different threads of teaching spread through the rich tapestry of understanding through the years.

My own connection with this energy remained strong; my Soul had been Attuned to it, and my path flowed beside its pathway, travelling always in sight of this precious energetic pulse.

In each incarnation I was able, always, to introduce more to its energy; to instruct more students in its ways and to ensure that the teaching of it continued, grew and remained within the human consciousness.

The energy of The Violet Flame had touched me. I, in turn, wished to touch it. Not to leave my mark, for this bright energy shines far beyond my own Light, but to ensure, through my work through the ages, that this energy was not forgotten, and that the Flame would continue to burn, brightened, if it were possible, through my work with it, and ensuring that while I lived, its light would not be allowed to falter.

The Energy Strengthens

As time passed, The Violet Flame of Transmutation was invoked repeatedly, and by many. And with each invocation, the energy of the Violet Flame strengthened. In the beginning the Flame held a power, certainly, one of great magnificence and majesty. Through its continued use by those who had achieved a mastery of their own power, the Flame became invested with the essence of their power, also.

As time passed, and those who used the Flame included those less powerful, in their individual Mastery, the essence of those Powerful Ones was accessed through the Flame, enhancing the energy of the Flame itself, so that those who called on it connected to not only the Flame, in its original glorious manifestation, but were also able to draw on the essence of those Beings of Power who had used it in ages past. This energy was powerful, indeed.

Because not all the energy came from the Flame itself, but included connection to other Beings of Power, it became possible for those less skilled to call upon the Flame, the safety of its use being enabled by the connection to the essence of other Beings, and not only the pure power of the Flame itself.

Let me explain, here, Beloved, that The Violet Flame, that pure vehicle of transmutation, is powerful in its own established right. It needs no supporting energy or Being to enable its full use. However, the use of that pure power by one who is not skilled and practised in the use of energy can be disturbing, to the energy of that Soul. Therefore, by invoking, also, the essence of Beings of Power, capable of holding the pure frequency of The Violet Flame – although that invocation is unspoken and unknown, save in the secret language of the Soul – one who is less skilled is able, safely, to invoke and use the Flame, to accomplish that which is intended, for the greater good and with no harm to all.

It is in this form of use that the Violet Flame of Transmutation has been employed in recent times. Those new (in this life, if not before!) to the experience of energy may safely be introduced to the vehicle of The Violet Flame as a means of transmutation. Here, the energy of the one who invokes it is often considerably less advanced and certainly less powerful than the energy of the Flame itself. Instead of a skilled and adept Being of Power invoking the Flame as a means of directing his own energy, any one who knows of it, irrespective of their own study or experience, may invoke the Flame as an essence more powerful than they, in sure and certain knowledge that this invocation and intention will bring about their desired result: transmutation of energy, through the power of the Violet Flame of Transmutation.

Invoke the Violet Flame

You have heard the history of it, now, Beloved, and you are free to use it. Call upon the energy of The Violet Flame in order to transmute whatever baser energies you do not require. Invoke the Flame for your self, invoke it for your space, for those with whom you work – in healing terms, Dear Ones, though the Flame may equally be employed in any work environment.

Wheresoever there is energy of a frequency lower than that which you would choose, use this Flame. Invoke it – that is, call upon it. Say "I now invoke the Violet Flame of Transmutation, if this be for the highest good of all". See it, burning through, transmuting and transforming, and know that it is true. It is safe for you to use, Beloved, I assure you. The many who have wielded this power through the ages provide you now with a protection from its raw energy. Whatever your understanding, the Flame, in this form, is safe for you to use. Do so, Dear One, trust your own power, and know that you can do this, for your benefit, and for the benefit of all.

Chapter Thirteen

(CHANNELLING FROM SAINT-GERMAIN)

The Energy Moves Forward

This, then, Dear One, is the foundation of the work that we are doing now. This original Flame, this Ancient energy – for it was in existence before my connection with it so long ago, remember; a truly primeval force – provides the support and underpinning of the new energies that flow in our time.

You are familiar, Dear One, with the rise in frequency of the Earth and all upon her; with the change in energy which enables, now, so much within the healing field. Of the gradual Awakening of Humanity to the greater energies, and wider vision that unfolds before you.

This has been, and still is, a gradual process. A little introduced here, a little more there; a new idea; an enhanced healing modality; a change in the process of connecting upward; an increase in awareness in all. This gradual unfoldment is still continuing, and will do so as Humanity continues to evolve and to grow to heights not yet experienced.

You can be part of this. Indeed, Dear One, you *are* part of this. Your connection with this book, with my words and energy held within its pages, and, through that, your connection to the Violet Flame, in all its aspects, links you to the ceaseless movement forward, upward, onward that you, and All, are experiencing now. As you become consciously aware, of my energy, and of these new teachings, so you carry that energy within you. You become a Flame yourself, holding the energy of the Violet Flame within your Being, and enabling the spreading of that energy to all.

New Aspects

With the changes in recent years has come the successful introduction of new energies; new aspects, of that which was familiar. In this way, the aspect of The Silver Violet Flame was introduced, bringing in to the combination of energy that was The Violet Flame, the Silver essence of the Divine Feminine, as this energy began to be accepted within the Whole.

In truth, Dear Ones, the frequency of the Divine Feminine was always present within the energy of the Violet Flame. Its only absence was in the consciousness of Humanity. As Humanity began to recognise, and to acknowledge the Female Aspect of Divinity, so the corresponding aspect within the Flame could also be acknowledged.

Its introduction was not, therefore, into the Flame, but into the awareness of those who invoked the Flame. The Flame has always been Whole; all aspects, all energies together. The appearance of change within the Flame is, then, more accurately explained as a change within Human Consciousness.

The Violet Flame Chakra

You may wonder, then, about the introduction of the Energy of the Violet Flame Chakra, and its associated healing tools, questioning whether this, too, has always been present, and appears to you simply through a transition in awareness.

This, Beloved, is indeed different. This is, indeed, new. An introduction to Humanity, as you reach a height in frequency not sustained for some long time.

Following the "introduction", or should I say, acceptance, of the Divine Feminine within the Silver

Violet Flame, other aspects of the Violet Flame began to be introduced.

White Fire

"White Fire" was a gift I bestowed upon my small Group towards our early time together. An essence, Flame of course, as the name suggests, which they were invited to employ to enable and assist healing. A short burst of this White Fire would clear and cleanse energy within a client.

It was not designed to replace the Violet Flame, and did not carry its full power. Its introduction was a gift to my faithful few. It carried power, and would be effective in its employment, but its greatest gift lay in the fact that it had been offered, and had been accepted.

This Group had gathered, under my instruction, to work together to assist the progress towards Ascension, of individuals within the Group, but, more importantly, of The Whole.

These dear Souls had made their commitment, before returning earthwards for this incarnation, to assist humanity, and the earth, in the Ascension process.

And this they did. Much work was accomplished through their assistance, and much gratitude extends to them for this important work.

By receiving the gift of White Fire, and by holding this frequency within their energy field, they enabled further awareness of higher aspects of a variety of familiar healing tools. This increased awareness allowed the further "introduction" of new tools and new modalities.

All worked together for the evolution of the Whole.

December 2012

With the significant shift in frequency following the December Solstice in 2012, many things changed. More people became aware of energy, and matters beyond the physical, and those already familiar with such matters, became more acutely, and most gloriously, so.

New healing processes were explored, new techniques refined, and at last the level of energy-work undertaken began to approach that which had been achieved in past times, when energies had flowed freely and Humanity had been moving joyously towards its full potential.

Now, in this time, with the increase in energetic frequency, it is possible to introduce new processes, new techniques, new aspects of old, familiar tools, and for Humanity to move forward from the stage that it was at so long ago.

Now, it is possible, for the evolution to continue.

The energy of the Violet Flame Chakra, and its associated Rescue Flames is part of that evolution.

Chapter Fourteen

(CHANNELLING FROM SAINT-GERMAIN)

Humanity's Evolution

The energy of the Violet Flame Chakra, then, is part of Humanity's progress. It is more than merely a new healing tool, a further technique, to be practised by skilled energy-workers.

It is a key to unlock Humanity's potential, to enable you, all, upon the Earth plane to Ascend, and to achieve that of which you, on Soul level, are all capable.

And this it will do. Received, now, upon the Earth, and held within the collective consciousness, the power of this energy, in all it aspects, has already begun healing, cleansing and clearing on a deep level. My encouragement that this work should spread is not, only, Dear Ones, that you should have more tools at your disposal, be able to offer more to those who come to you, but, more importantly, that this healing should continue, cleansing, clearing and transmuting all within you.

There is much darkness at this time; this you know. It is not a darkness from without, but rather a final emerging of the darkness that has been held within you, that has gradually, over time, become ingrained.

Such deeply held energy requires tools of great power, love, wisdom and light to clear it. The energy of the Violet Flame Chakra offers such tools.

Spread This Energy

Spread this energy, then, Dear Ones. Let it flow. Share it, speak of it, hold its vibration within your Being. And as you do so, you free not only yourselves, but the All.

The power of these tools is not only for cleansing. This is their purpose, now, at this time, for this is the greatest need. While the tarnish is present, the gold cannot gleam. And you are Golden, Dear Ones. Golden, and shining, and you should be seen as such.

But for now, your light is dimmed, and the energy of the Violet Flame Chakra can re-kindle that light, strengthen your own inner Flame, and allow you to burn brightly once again.

And then, Beloveds, when all has been cleansed, when all that is not pure has been released, transmuted, changed into a higher form, then, Most Dear Ones, the energy of the Violet Flame can return to her original purpose: that of illumination and inspiration.

Then, Beloveds, there will be no need to sit within a Sanctuary, hidden within a Temple, in order to experience the energy of the Violet Flame. With the Awakening of your Violet Flame Chakra, you will hold that energy within you. And that Flame will be present in greater strength and majesty than it was before, for now, you hold awareness of it in all its aspects. And as your awareness grows, so does your understanding of it.

The Flame of Life

For this Flame, Dear Ones, is the Flame of Life itself. Living fire, present throughout the ages, in a different form, but now, with the energy of Ascension growing within your Beings, you can hold, perceive, experience and marvel at the Whole of this Flame of Life, in all its multitudinous aspects.

As you grow, so your awareness of this Glorious Flame grows, and as you draw its energy into your Being, so your growth continues. This Flame is your energy, and also your goal. Connect with it, breathe it, use it, and as you do so, that very use enhances its own energy within you, allowing your experience of it to become ever more profound.

This is the Gift that is bestowed on you. Not, merely a healing tool of great power and great strength, but an energy of transformation, inspiration and illumination.

Light this Heavenly Flame within your Being, Dear One. Let its Light shine, for all to see. Transform yourself, and, in so doing, enable the continuing transformation and evolution of the Whole. Let Humanity become, as it proceeds upon its journey forward, illuminated by the Light of the Living Violet Flame.

The goal is not yet reached, but the path, now, is sure. Embracing the energy of the Violet Flame, and, through its power, allowing the transmuting and releasing of all that no longer serves and then, being led by its Living Light, following the guidance that it gives, you will reach your goal. You will become, each one of you, a Living Violet Flame, and Humanity will move into a new level of existence and experience.

This is your Ascension, Beloveds, your journey beyond that which Humanity has experienced before. The energy of the Violet Flame is your gift, to enable you to reach that goal. It is a great gift. Receive it, celebrate it, and enjoy. The journey awaits, Beloved. Travel with me towards your own Becoming."

Chapter Fifteen

Continuing Growth

What a journey this is becoming! And how exciting to be involved in work that, potentially, has such an impact on Humanity's evolution. We are blessed indeed!

Saint-Germain's words made a great deal of sense. I can see that this is not just a healing tool – powerful though it is; it is in fact something much greater. And the idea of the Violet Flame being able to return to its original purpose – that of illumination and inspiration – resonates deeply with me.

Our work within the subtle energetic realms is certainly changing. Our ability to perceive and connect with higher, and finer, energies continues to increase. The manifestation of our thoughts – both positive and negative! – is becoming more rapid. We have been told, for some time now, that such changes would become evident; and they are.

The Power of the Violet Flame Chakra

A recent experience with a client confirmed for me the magic of the energy of the Violet Flame Chakra. She was experiencing a Reiki treatment (although both of us knew that there would be much more than Reiki flowing within our space). I was aware of an energetic block within her physical form which would benefit from being released. I mentally asked which of the potential tools would be appropriate for such a release. The answer came that the Rescue Flames would be of greatest benefit.

In order to use them effectively, a particular sacred space should be set up, and then a mantra recited before the energies are brought in.

My client had no (conscious) idea what I was doing. She did not know that I planned to enable a release, and she had no knowledge of the energy of the Violet Flame Chakra, or what was needed to engage such energy.

She had been lying silently, immersed in the treatment. I mentally created the sacred space, and was just approaching the completion of silently reciting the mantra – in other words, this was the point at which the energy had built to its peak before the Flames were introduced.

At that point she said "Wow". "Oh, Wow. That's amazing." At no other time within the treatment did she speak.

When the treatment was complete, we shared our impressions of the session. I explained to her what I had been engaged in when she spoke, and how magical it was that she should experience, and respond to, the energy at that moment. Although I had seen the Flames "in action" before, this further manifestation was quite special.

Infinite Rescue Flames

And the fantastic story of the Rescue Flames continues to evolve:

While writing the first draft of this book, I heard from Liz that she and Mesheril had received more Flames. Liz shared these latest arrivals with us at our second "Stage Two" Day in July this year. And in the course of that day, a further Flame was "received".

On this occasion it was someone other than Liz who became aware of the energy, and Liz encouraged us to trust our intuition: if we felt we were connecting to a new Flame, with a new colour, Presence and purpose, then we should trust that, and allow the energy to flow.

At the same workshop Saint-Germain spoke, also encouraging us to trust any guidance we received with regard to new Rescue Flames.

I shared with those present his words earlier in this book, about the Feminine (Silver Violet) aspect of the Violet Flame always being present, and it being a change in our consciousness which enabled our recognition of it, rather than a new aspect coming into being.

We all felt that the same was true of the "new" Rescue Flames. It was likely that there were, already, an infinite number of Flames – or aspects to the Violet Flame - each aspect with its own colour, Presence and purpose. Any awareness that any one of us had of a "new" Flame, was an indication of Humanity's consciousness rising to a level where that vibration could be experienced, rather than the sudden creation of a new Rescue Flame.

This has since been borne out, with more Flames being recognised, some by Liz and Mesheril, and some by others. We are all opening to the acceptance of our ability to recognise these new aspects of the energy of the Violet Flame.

Chapter Sixteen

Channelling is Changing

Even without having received the Awakening of their Violet Flame Chakra, many of those sensitive to subtle vibrations are becoming more tuned in to the frequency of energy at this level. As a consequence, their awareness during giving or receiving healing is changing and evolving.

In addition, the process of Channelling is becoming much more widely experienced, as more people allow themselves to receive and to communicate thoughts, feelings and energy from Higher Beings.

As mentioned in Chapter Six, the process of Channelling used to require the Channel to move into a state of trance, losing consciousness and with it the knowledge and memory of what was said and shared. This approach is less common these days.

I remember, soon after the Millennium, in a Channelling session with a client, the client asked why it was no longer necessary for the Channel to "disappear" – move into a deep trance state – during the process. The answer that was given was that in time past, the difference between the frequency of the Higher Being and the frequency of the Channel was so great, that effective connection could only be achieved if some of the energy of the Channel withdrew, and some of the energy of the Higher Being literally "came into" the body of the Channel.

At that time (2000), with the rise in frequency of the Earth and those upon her, the difference in frequency between the two Beings was reducing. It was possible, therefore, in a greater number of situations, for the connection to be made while the Channel was still present.

Consider now, then, how much higher our frequency has become, with the passing of more time (frequencies rising all the while) combined with the significant leap forward and upward at the Winter Solstice in 2012. It is not surprising that Channelling now can be effected through a subtle merging of vibrations – the Higher and the Lower – with the Channel remaining fully present – though in a blissful state of love and light – throughout.

In addition to the process of Channelling becoming easier and more fluid, more people are, literally, opening to Channelling.

No longer is it the preserve of special individuals, offering this process on separate, rare occasions. Many healers find themselves Channelling, as part of their treatments, allowing words of guidance, often accompanied by higher frequency energy, to flow towards their clients.

Workshop students, too, are encouraged to try their hand at Channelling, either vocally, or, more usually, through written means. By allowing themselves to surrender to the energy which surrounds them, they often surprise themselves by writing words whose wisdom they know is not their own.

I, personally, feel that we are all moving upward – indeed I am sure of it – and this upward movement allows us to connect more easily, and sometimes unconsciously with the Higher Realms.

Different Grades of Channelling

I have my own personal "grading" system of the higher-communication work I do.

The highest grade is what I would term "full Channelling". This is when I allow myself to be immersed within the energy of a Greater Being (usually, now, Saint-Germain). I am fully aware of his energy, and his "thoughts" connect with mine, to the point where I can no longer "not speak", and his words then flow, to be heard by those present. This is a glorious connection, and one which – I feel – I could remain in endlessly. It is blissful, powerful and loving.

However, as other Channels will attest, while I might like to remain in this frequency for hours at a time, holding such a presence requires my energy, and if the connection is held for too long, then the energy expended manifests as tiredness on the physical level. While my mind and higher aspects might desire a longer connection, the wellbeing of my physical body dictates that such connections should be limited to an hour or so at any one time.

Typing the words of Saint-Germain require a similar level of connection and immersion. Slightly less, as the fingers must be free to move, but still the connection cannot comfortably be maintained for more than an hour.

Continuing down the "grading" scale, is the degree of connection required to do a Reading, using Tarot or other tools of Divination. Here, no immersion is necessary, though I am aware that the messages I convey, and the words I use, are not my own. The process is clearly guided.

Next on down is what I term a "guided conversation". Here, the process may begin as a normal conversation, but, particularly if matters of guidance or spirituality are discussed, it may become apparent that what is being shared is no longer just my own view, and limited wisdom, but includes the input, and often the energy, of a Higher Being.

I feel that, as the frequencies continue to rise, both individually and collectively, such "guided conversations", and, indeed, spontaneous full Channellings, will become more frequent and more commonplace.

Daily Magic

Already many people have come to accept "magic" into their daily lives: infusing water with crystals, clearing spaces, blessing food; seeking guidance, in one form or another, and turning to the "alternative" practitioners as often as the conventional ones.

Imagine, if we were to fully embrace all the gifts and attributes that we have: Sending Reiki forward to smooth our day, consciously employing the Law of

Attraction to draw to ourselves that which we choose; trusting our own inner guidance system: through a rise or fall in our energy levels it indicates to us our degree of alignment with the Divine; and invoking the energy of the Violet Flame to cleanse and transmute all that no longer serves.

And, in addition to our own "powers", we have a vast team of Angels, Archangels, Goddesses and Ascended Masters who can be called upon to add "oomph" to our endeavours. Struggling with a legal battle? Call on Pallas Athena for resolution. Looking for love? Ask Quan Yin, Lady Nada or Mary Magdalene to open your heart. Need money? Abundantia or Lakshmi can assist you here. And if you don't know the relevant Deity for the job, then just ask!

All the help we need is accessible to us, if we will only remember to use it.

Love, Light and Joy

And if we do, then how easily and smoothly our life flows. Then, we are truly "in the flow" moving within that ceaseless current of love, light, joy and abundance that is always present, if only we will cease our determined struggle, and Allow.

In this regard, the energy of the Violet Flame Chakra is a valuable tool. The Awakening of that energy within our Being raises our frequency, and this enables easier and more smooth connection with the Agents of the Divine. The ability to transmute all that does not serve enables us to free ourselves, to release the old, heavy energy that we have held within our Being, and this in turn, allows our frequency to rise still further.

At that higher level, connection becomes even easier, energy flowing more freely; clarity of vision also comes, and greater insight and understanding.

It is not by chance that the location of the Violet Flame Chakra is on our brow. By increasing our energy in that part of our Being we enable higher vision – bringing greater clarity – and a greater awareness of higher things.

As Saint-Germain said "Look up, Beloveds. For that, then, is the direction in which you will move."

And as Humanity continues its collective shift towards Ascension any tool which enables us to move further "Up" is of immense value. In the energy of the Living Violet Flame, with all its potential, we are blessed with a very great gift indeed.

Addendum

Since writing the material for this book, the Violet Flame Chakra work has evolved further. Indeed – I feel it will continue to evolve, and all we can ever do is observe and comment on it in its current form.

This book gives you the story of the journey up to the summer of 2014. There is more…

Leith Hill

In September 2014 Edwin led a further workshop focussed around Leith Hill, in Surrey: the location of the Violet Flame Chakra of the Earth. The day included a visit to Leith Hill itself, and work connecting to the energy there.

The Violet Flame Chakra of the Earth was awakened during the workshop I attended in November 2013.

Since that time its power had been growing, fed by those who were working with the energy of the Violet Flame Chakra.

Our work in September, as we stood on Leith Hill, guided our attention down into the Chakra itself, and then directed the energy of the Violet Flame Chakra of the Earth up, through the hill, and out to the whole planet. Those present recognised that the power of the Chakra increased as we did this, and we knew that a change had taken place.

It felt as if the Chakra had now moved into its second phase. It had been Awakened, and had grown in power, and now it was established, and able to share that power with those around it.

Until that time the Chakra had been mainly receiving – fed by the energy and attention of those who worked with it. Now, it would give also; others would draw on its strength and power, and be nourished and supported by the energy that the Chakra emitted.

Receiving Your Own Awakening

I have written in this book about Awakenings, and receiving Awakenings. Saint-Germain has encouraged you to receive and experience the energy of the Violet

Flame Chakra. You may now be seeking your own Awakening.

How can this be done?

An Awakening can be done on a one-to-one basis, but I have found it to be more effective when carried out in the high frequency of a group or workshop. The combined energy of all those present enables greater healing and a more powerful transition.

I offer regular Awakening workshops, and these are open to all. No previous healing or therapy training is required to receive and work with the energy of the Violet Flame Chakra.

Once you have received your own Awakening, you are able to pass the process on to others. Anyone who has been Awakened can carry out further Awakenings. Indeed, the number of people regularly offering these Awakening workshops continues to grow.

Details of my workshops, including Awakenings, Stage Two Days (now called The Evolution of the Violet Flame Chakra workshops) and visits to Leith Hill to connect with the energy there, can be found on my website: www.violetflamechakra.com.

I would be delighted to share this special energy with you, and encourage you to experience the unique vibration of your own Awakened Violet Flame Chakra.

Printed in the United States
By Bookmasters